SHE WARRIOR

Rosalinda Rivera

...to the brave warriors
who refuse to stop fighting.

She Warrior
Rosalinda Rivera
https://rosalinda.live

First Edition: 2022
Copyright © 2022 by Rosalinda Rivera

ISBN# 979-8-218-20955-1

Annandale Publishing
P.O. BOX 13526
RICHMOND, VA 23225

1 2 3 4 5 6   25 24 23 22

SHE Warrior

Rosalinda
Rivera

ANNANDALE

The wicked run away when no one is chasing them, but the godly are as bold as lions.
Proverbs 28:1, NLT

Bold Like a Warrior

A bold warrior is willing to get things done despite the fear and risks. In Proverbs, Solomon spoke that the wicked run from their problems, but the godly are bold as lions. Many want to run when issues arise.

Some situations are so severe, we may wish to manifest a cave to crawl into and never come out. If we are constantly on the run, we garner a victim mentality of inferiority and weakness. Have you felt that way? Warrior, today I speak to your heart --*You are not weak! You are not inferior! You are more than enough!*

YOU ARE MORE THAN ENOUGH! IT'S TIME TO FACE FORWARD, CHIN UP AND HEAD HIGH.

It's time to face forward, chin up and head high. Declare the goodness of God in your life. Confront whatever you need to face with the boldness God gives you. 'Cause honey, today it's time to roar like the true God-fearing, devil-defeating lioness that you are!

Be strong and courageous. Do not be afraid or terrified because of them, for the LORD your God goes with you; he will never leave you nor forsake you.
Deuteronomy 31:6, NIV

Fierce Like a Warrior

Today, fierce warrior, praise the Lord with all of your soul! The Lord God goes with you wherever you go (Joshua 1:9). He never has and never will leave you or forsake you.

God sees the needs of His people way before those needs become a reality.

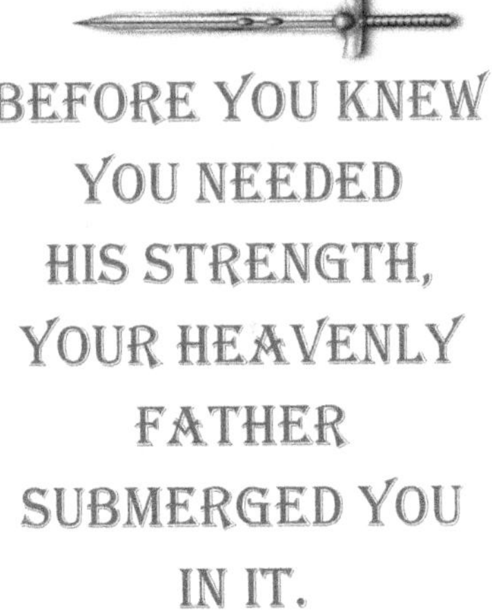

Before you knew you needed His strength, your Heavenly Father submerged you in it. Even when the unknown is before you, remember you are ferocious and created for such a time as this.

In life, you won't always get what you think you deserve -- but you will get what you confront and contend for. Fierce Warrior, fight and never forget how the mighty commander of the heavenly host is leading your charge.

Rally to us wherever you hear the sound of the trumpet. Our God will fight for us.
Nehemiah 4:20, NRSV

Build Like a Warrior

Construction starts long before the laying of brick and mortar. Building begins with a blueprint, with planning and preparation. Nehemiah took fifty-two days to erect the city walls of Jerusalem, but before he announced his plans to recruit workers, he secretly surveyed the land. He did not come unprepared.

At times, building like a warrior even means rebuilding what was destroyed by past generations to prepare for future generations.

Be proud that you can say, I *am a warrior, and I will construct and create a better future*. Nothing you are fighting and building for today is in vain, no matter how much the enemy may try to confuse you. Be encouraged.

> WITH THE SWORD OF THE SPIRIT IN ONE HAND AND FAITH IN THE OTHER, YOU DID NOT COME UNPREPARED.

With the Sword of the Spirit in one hand and faith in the other, do not forget that God builds the house and wins the battles!

Great is the LORD and most worthy of praise; his greatness no one can fathom. One generation commends your works to another; they tell of your mighty acts.
Psalms 145:3-4, NIV

Live Like a Warrior

Today I proclaim that I will call upon the Lord, for He is worthy of praise (Psalm 18:3). I will live each day honoring my Lord and Savior. My life shall reflect His love, grace, and forgiveness.

I will show kindness in situations that may be unexpected, unfair, or unjust. I choose to honor the Lord in how I live my life so that it may be a testimony to others.

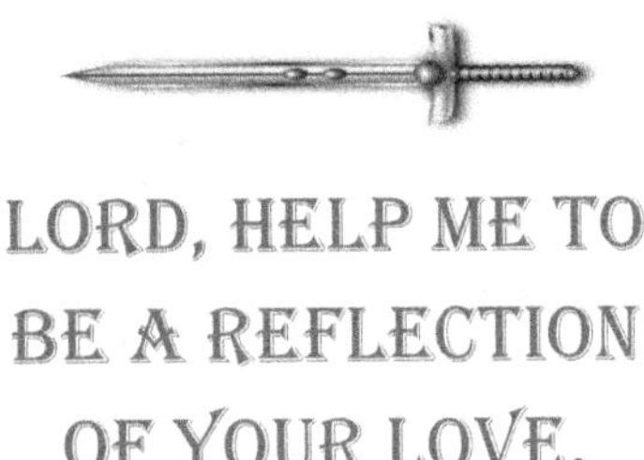

As a warrior, my standards will be high. In doing so, I will stand out from the crowd because I will not lower my standards. Even though my flesh may be tired, I will fight the good fight. I will not allow the enemy to conquer my mind or my emotions.

Dear Lord, help me to be a reflection of Your love. My prayer is that when people look at me, they will see the heart of Jesus and the grace of our Lord.

Your word is a lamp to
my feet And a light to my
path.
Psalm 119:105, NKJV

Believe Like a Warrior

To build our faith, we must speak out loud what God sees in us. Today, allow yourself to declare the truth of God's light in your life into your atmosphere. Marry this moment of belief to your determination to have faith in your God.

Declare today:

I am anointed to win, to overcome, to accomplish. I believe the promises that God has made to me as a believer. I am confident that God will finish the good work He has begun in me. My talents, gifts, and dreams are all because God has equipped me to achieve my goals for His glory. What He has birthed in me will come to pass. When I see myself the way God does, His connections will come my way.

Today I declare the windows of Heaven will open over me. I praise God that His Word is a lamp unto my feet and a light unto my path. I believe because God is faithful.

For God has not given us a spirit of fear, but of power and of love and of a sound mind.
2 Timothy 1:7, NKJV

Boss Like a Warrior

To be a *boss* is to "be in charge of someone, something, or have authority in a situation."[1] Have you found circumstances, others' comments, or things beyond your control are taking control over you, becoming the boss of *you*?

Today is your reminder of how God has given you the strength of a sound mind over your life. Let God overcome your thoughts so others do not force their plots and plans onto you.

Instead, stand firm and take your position of being the boss over your own life.

Declare today: *I am strong, loyal, trustworthy, committed, innovative, and I am a leader.*

Yes! You are a leader. God didn't put you in the circles and environments you are in by chance. Leading is an act of influence. You are responsible for the impact you carry. Let God's light emanate through you.

*If you find honey,
eat just enough—
too much of it, and you
will vomit.
Proverbs 25:16,* NIV

Eat Like a Warrior

Food is such a touchy topic. Many of us have a love/hate relationship with eating; there are just way too many delicious things out there. Our bodies become addicted to the satisfaction of sugary treats. You may not have a problem with lust or alcohol, but what of the addictive traits of food? There is no need for guilt today; simply encouragement to be attentive to what you consume.

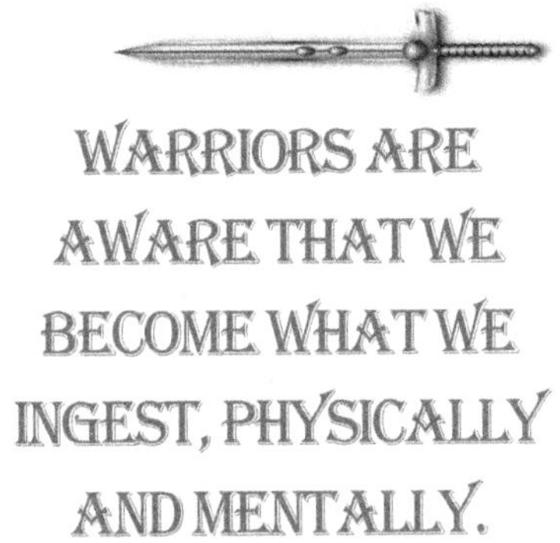

Warriors are aware that we become what we ingest, physically and mentally. God provides animals & plants for our bodies, and we have endless amenities, entertainment opportunities, and activities of which to indulge. Yet, anything that keeps us from God and takes us from taking care of our bodies works against our life's purpose. We must balance how we eat and in what we indulge and engage ourselves, keeping Christ as our center. Let's allow our Heavenly Father to ordain our steps so we properly care for the holy vessel He gave us.

To them God has chosen to make known among the Gentiles the glorious riches of this mystery, which is Christ in you, the hope of glory. Colossians 1:27, NIV

Hope Like a Warrior

Because I put my trust in You, even though my past is full of failures, I will not stop. I will not give in. My heart sings praises to Your name, and my heart is at ease. When I have no words to pray, when my emotions are exhausted, I will say the name of Jesus. You took my shame and all of my pain to the cross. I am set free. I am blameless. Today I feel Your loving arms wrapping around my imperfection and making me whole. I can believe again, trust again, hope again; for Christ is my hope of glory.

WHEN I HAVE NO WORDS TO PRAY, WHEN MY EMOTIONS ARE EXHAUSTED, I WILL SAY THE NAME OF JESUS.

He will cover you with his pinions, and under his wings you will find refuge; his faithfulness is a shield and buckler.
Psalm 91:4, CSB

Accelerate Like a Warrior

My plane is sitting on the tarmac runway at the airport, where it has been for over thirty minutes. The air conditioning isn't working, and I am going to miss a huge conference keynote event. *Other than that, I am fine.*

Hundreds of women are counting on me to arrive at a particular time. *Desperate* and *hopeless* describe my situation well. Have you ever wanted to speed things up?

Suddenly, I feel a trembling under my feet. The engines begin to crank up. Within minutes, the wheels turn, the plane gathers speed, and we finally take off.

Lesson learned: We cannot accelerate in God's assignment if worry consumes us.

Allow God to take over. Soon you will fly above the clouds, soaring under the wings of the Almighty.

But the fruit of the Spirit is love, joy, peace, forbearance, kindness, goodness, faithfulness, gentleness and self-control. Against such things there is no law. Galatians 5:22-23, NIV

Cultivate Like a Warrior

You became a life-giving garden when you received Jesus Christ as your Lord and Savior. Kneeling before God, your heart becomes fertile ground to be cultivated by faithfulness to your Heavenly Father. From your life springs gentleness, goodness, joy, kindness, love, patience, peace, and self-control (Galatians 5:22-23).

Anything that yields fruit must first be exposed to the foundational principle of cultivation; preparing a suitable environment for growth is as essential to our spiritual lives as it is to agriculture.

The beauty of your life, Warrior, comes from turning over each moment to make it fertile. The hardest of moments become rich soil when the Lord cultivates your circumstances. Do not allow your surroundings or past to invite worms of bitterness to damage what God produces in your life. Allow your fruit to be a legacy to bless others.

> THE HARDEST OF MOMENTS BECOME RICH SOIL WHEN THE LORD CULTIVATES YOUR CIRCUMSTANCES.

Now to him who is able to do above and beyond all that we ask or think according to the power that works in us.
Ephesians 3:20, CSB

Finish Like a Warrior

Warrior, you have already gone through so much in life. Just think of everything God has helped you through. Remember the moments you have prayed and received answers to those prayers?

Even in the smallest of needs, God has been there. Your journey will look different than others. Your walk in life, circumstances, and perspective will not be the same as another's.

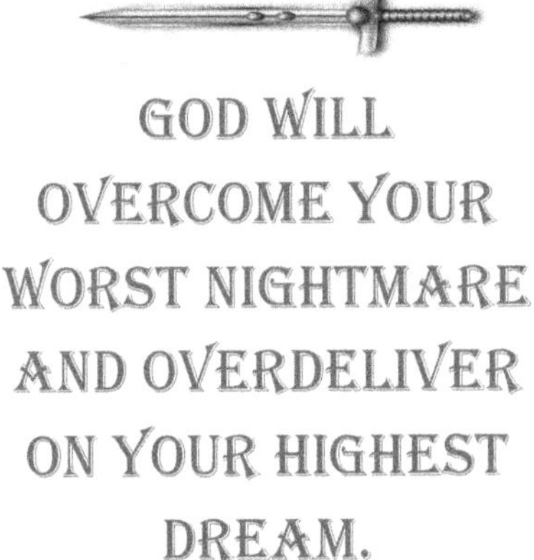

Regardless of what obstacles are in front of you, finish like the warrior you are. The enemy will not defeat you. Advance with confidence, knowing God will overcome your worst nightmare and overdeliver on your highest dream.

Therefore, since we are surrounded by such a great cloud of witnesses, let us throw off everything that hinders and the sin that so easily entangles. And let us run with perseverance the race marked out for us, fixing our eyes on Jesus, the pioneer and perfecter of faith.
Hebrews 12:1-2b, NIV

Focus Like a Warrior

It's common to be distracted by our ever-growing lists of things to do and get discouraged when we fail to accomplish them. The weight of never-ending responsibilities is a constant reminder to keep our eyes on God.

When we desire to please Him in all we do, we are more motivated to focus and finish. After all, we must give God the glory in everything; no assignment is too mundane to do well for God.

Handling the tasks before us with excellence is another form of worship to our Heavenly Father. Turn your focus on completing today's duties for God and by His strength. He is your source and strength; nothing can detain you from moving forward.

Today, my dear Warrior, stay on course and keep your emphasis on Him. Allow your devotion to be the incense of worship unto our Heavenly Father while finishing the tasks before you.

Praise be to the Lord my rock, who trains my hands for war, my fingers for battle.

Psalms 144:1, NIV

Discipline Like a Warrior

You must endure the training to fight and win battles. As a young boy serving King Saul, David learned to be skillful before defeating the mighty Philistine giant, Goliath (1 Samuel 17). Reading your Bible and gaining knowledge will not complete your equipping; you must actively apply what you know (2 Timothy 3:16-17).

Knowledge, understanding, prayer, and faith in action are the training program to prepare you for the fight. Such requires daily discipline in communion with God. We cannot become knowledge-only warriors; instead, we are to be mighty women who train in Spirit and truth. In such time with the Lord, He trains your hands for war and your heart for victory.

Today, begin to discipline yourself with God's nature, seeking Him always and gaining His Word's revelation. When the storms come, your training will bring you survival and revival.

To the Jews who had believed him, Jesus said, 'If you hold to my teaching, you are really my disciples. Thenyou will know the truth, and the truth will set you free.'"
John 8:31-32, NIV

Mentor Like a Warrior

Heavenly Father, thank You for sending mentors into my life. May You continue to bring those who can help me when I waver in my faith. Holy Spirit, guide my life and surround me with wise counsel. Your teachings, Your Holy Word, Your divine Holy Spirit is the beacon towards truth in a world where lies threaten the awareness of You.

Today I declare myself a warrior for Your Kingdom with humility in my heart. Being obedient to Your guidance, I am confident as I walk in truth through faith. As Your Word states, the truth will free me from the enemies' oppression. Thank You for being my beacon, guiding me through this fantastic journey.

"For I know the plans I have for you," declares the LORD, *"plans to prosper you and not to harm you, plans to give you hope and a future."*
Jeremiah 29:11, NIV

Defeat Like a Warrior

Dear warrior, remember you are *not* the defeated one. You are the daughter of Jehovah God, who already sent His Son to defeat the works of the enemy against your life (1 John 4:4).

A mighty warrior comes against the enemy's attacks, however they may manifest. God's plans over you are far greater than any pain along your journey. Begin to count your blessings as you go about your day.

Every moment you are grateful for what God has given you is another defeat against the darts the enemy hurls your way (1 Corinthians 15:57). Even the brave sometimes allow hurt and frustration to make us quick to dwell on our woes instead of our blessings. Because you are a warrior, it is time to stand up and proceed with gratitude for what God has given, for there is hope for a future that is simply divine.

Place your eyes upon the Lord today.

He who offers a sacrifice of thanksgiving honors Me; And to him who orders his way aright. I shall show the salvation of God.
Psalms 50:23, NASB

Honor Like a Warrior

We honor God through our love and obedience, but honor is not reserved only for our Lord. The Apostle Paul tells us to "honor one another" above ourselves, devoting ourselves to each other "in love" (Romans 12:10).

Honoring another person does not mean you must become a martyr; genuine esteem shows through our patience, kindness, and the other attributes of love listed in 1 Corinthians 13:4-8.

We express admiration for those over us, and devotion to those we are meant to protect. Honor shines out to everyone around us as we show favor and respect, even when we disagree. Like the return of fruit to the sower, there is a reward to those who give honor.

Today, where can you place seeds of honor? Allow your fruit to speak loudly for you, respectful Warrior. Let what comes out of you in beauty speak louder than any word expressed through your lips.

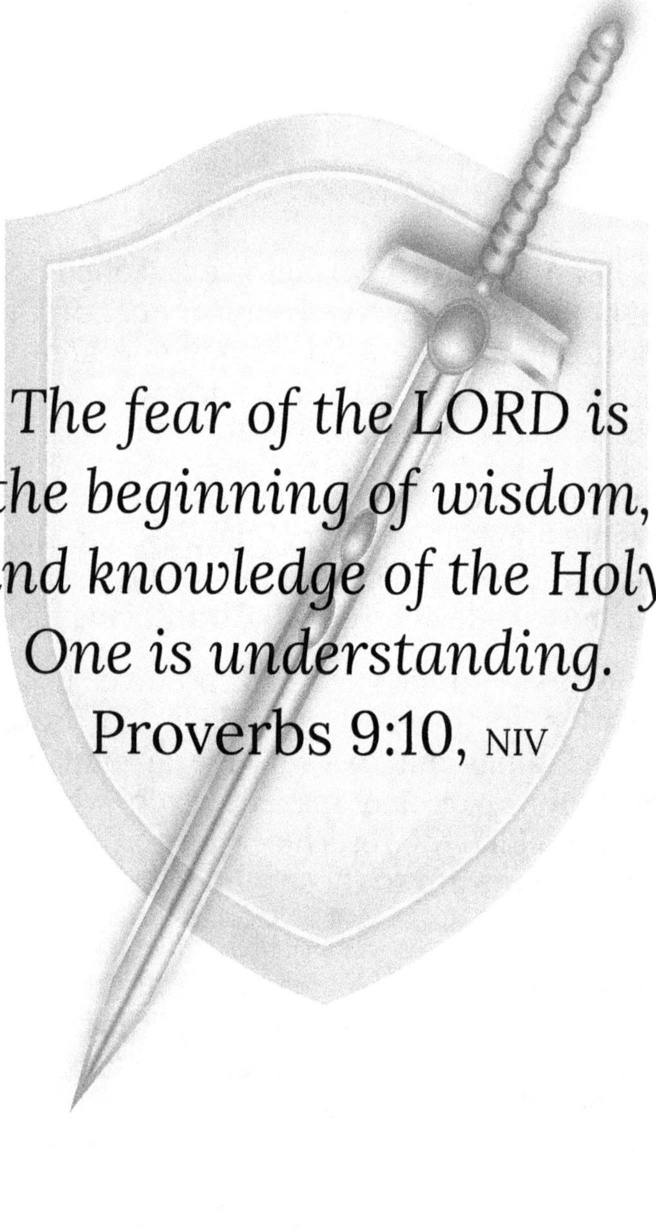

The fear of the LORD is the beginning of wisdom, and knowledge of the Holy One is understanding.
Proverbs 9:10, NIV

Learn Like a Warrior

Wisdom comes from lessons learned through life experiences. We are the students of life's journey. The beauty of learning from your Creator comes from deep intimacy with Him; trusting that He knows best.

If you see a child about to put a paperclip into an electrical socket, won't you rush to remove the danger?

We don't always recognize the harm behind an innocent decision – but God does. He knows and sees all and gears us through dangerous circumstances if we will listen and learn.

Strong and intelligent Warrior, never stop learning and leaning into the wisdom our Heavenly Father gives through His Word. Be His lifelong learner.

Do you not know that you are God's temple and that God's Spirit dwells in you? If anyone destroys God's temple, God will destroy him. For God's temple is holy, and you are that temple.

1 Corinthians 3:16-17, ESV

Exercise Like a Warrior

In the age in which we live, there is much said about our personal "rights." Why would Paul speak to us in First Corinthians about taking care of our temple if we are free to mistreat our bodies?

While a Christ-follower has the authority to cast out a spirit of infirmity, we are not entitled to cause illness or injury through our own neglect. You are the temple of the Holy Spirit. You must protect and care for your physical health along with your mental and spiritual self. Exercise and nutrition are not the only ways to stay healthy.

PRAYER, THE WORD, AND FELLOWSHIP GIVE US CONFIDENCE, JOY, AND GRATITUDE.

Prayer, the Word, fellowshipping with God gives us confidence, joy, and gratitude. Medical science proves the physiological benefits of positive attitudes[2] -- a simple concept but challenging to accomplish. Exercise mind, body, and spirit, allowing no weakness for the enemy to exploit.

Give your burdens
to the LORD,
and he will take
care of you.
He will not permit the
godly to slip and fall.
Psalm 55:22, NLT

Heal Like a Warrior

Healing, true healing, often takes time. Our God is thorough, desiring to bring us to wholeness physically, mentally, emotionally, and spiritually. After all, how many times did King David have the most intimate and intense conversations with God during his pain?

The Psalms are full of those moments of seeking and surrendering that must come before the breakthrough and the blessings.

Dear Warrior, do not rush your current season of healing; give in to the process.

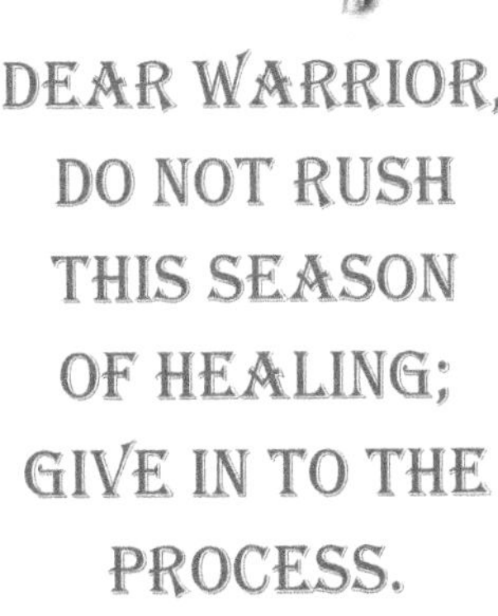

God has an ultimate plan for your wellness in every area of your life. He knows what you need to get through the journey of life. Lean into Him and allow His rest, peace, direction, and wisdom to be your lead.

The Spirit of God has made me, And the breath of the Almighty gives me life.
Job 33:4, NASB

Breathe Like a Warrior

I will call upon the Lord, who is worthy to be praised. As I call on You, Lord, I will inhale all of Your goodness, releasing my stress, challenges, difficulties, and struggles.

Today, I present a fully-yielded woman before You, oh, Lord. In the stillness of my heart, I will feel the warmth and power of the Holy Spirit engulfing my soul and calming my thoughts. Today is not yesterday. Today is today.

Your Spirit, oh, Lord, is what has made me. You breathed in me the breath of life. Thank You for Your wondrous work that created me into Your perfect image.

Today, I commit to breathe of Your presence to stay present with Your nature.

"*For as he thinks in his heart, so is he.*"
Proverbs 23:7, NKJV

Champion Like a Warrior

How is your vision? Being a champion requires you to see yourself as a champion. It also requires speaking life to your body, thoughts, and surroundings. A true champion prepares for the race with more than strength and endurance training. No matter how hard an athlete trains, mental preparedness can inevitably be the tipping point to success or failure.

Do you picture yourself winning? Like an Olympian, you must encounter each day knowing you are in front, clearing the hurdles, and winning the race. You face your giants and win your battles because God formed you in His already perfect image. He created you knowing you will face hurdles, yet gave you the strength to overcome them physically and mentally.

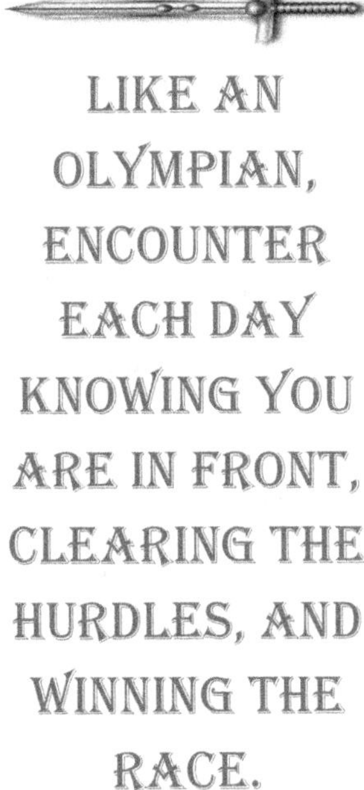

Today, see yourself as the winner.

"She is clothed with
strength and dignity;
she can laugh at the days
to come.
She speaks with wisdom,
and faithful instruction is
on her tongue.
She watches over the
affairs of her household
and does not eat the bread
of idleness."
Proverbs 31:25-27, NIV

Forge Like a Warrior

You did not create a quitter in me, my God. You made me in Your perfected image. I will forge forward until the job gets done. I will not quit praying for my family. I will not cease declaring Your goodness in the land of the living. I will not stop fighting for a better future, a healthy life, and a sustainable lifestyle. Everything I have is because You gave it to me. In gratitude, I will always give You the glory in all I accomplish in Your Name.

You created me as a warrior, and a warrior does not give up. I will move forward without looking back. My past is a part of my journey, but it will not determine my future. Thank You for choosing me, oh Lord, to be Your warrior, fighting for what lies ahead and for those around me. You clothed me with strength and dignity; You gave me wisdom to speak and guide my affairs. You, oh Lord, choose me for this journey, and I am honored to be called Yours.

My people are destroyed for lack of knowledge.
Hosea 4:6a, NKJV

Educated Like a Warrior

God did not create humanity to shrink behind the guise of ignorance. If anything, His children are to become leaders, and teachers – "the head and not the tail" of any situation (Deuteronomy 28:13).

How are we to become front-runners of His righteousness and creative ideas unless we grow and tend to our understanding of Him? Are you invested in your development?

BEAT BACK THE ROOT OF DARKNESS & BRING THE ENEMY'S SCHEMES TO RUBBLE.

To build your knowledge and strengthen your bond, you must dive into His Word and educate yourself. God's Holy Word is full of weapons and tools to battle and build, both in the natural and the spiritual realms. The enemy tries to distract with his lies, but he is defeated each time a warrior wields the Sword of the Spirit – the Word of God. When scripture comes to the forefront of your prayers, you beat back the root of darkness and bring the enemy's schemes to rubble (Matthew 4).

Today, arm yourself, using the weapon of the Word to your advantage in battle.

For God did not give us a spirit of timidity or cowardice or fear, but [He has given us a spirit] of power and of love and of sound judgment and personal discipline [abilities that result in a calm, well-balanced mind and self-control].
2 Timothy 1:7, AMP

Fearless Like a Warrior

Dear Warrior, today, declare boldness over your mind, body, and spirit. Fear is the unease over the unknown. Do not let it send you into hiding.

A true warrior of God meets challenges head-on. Confront what is in front of you and inside of you with God commanding your ship.

Today, strong one, declare 2 Timothy 1:7 over your life – you possess a spirit of power, love, and a sound mind. The debilitating fear that may try to control you did not come from God. He gives all that is good, beneficial, and strong.

Remember, you have the power over all circumstances. Issues and painful events in life only gain power over you to the degree you allow.

Today, abandon that evil grip and allow God's charge over your life, fearless Warrior.

But I discipline my body
and keep it under control,
lest after preaching to
others
I myself should be
disqualified.
1 Corinthians 9:27, ESV

Model Like a Warrior

A true leader knows she is only as strong as those around her. She is a model of integrity and wisdom; she knows how to cultivate the strengths of others. A director sets a foundation of trust and respect, allowing her squad to operate in their unique strengths while working collectively in a common pursuit.

Part of why you are on this earth is to lead others to Christ. You do not need to be behind a pulpit, on a stage, or in a powerful societal position to be a leader. Be yourself. Stay open to being an instrument in God's Kingdom for His glory.

As a mother, you are leading your children. As an employee or owner, you guide coworkers or staff. When someone is in mourning, you are an example of empathy and compassion. What you carry inside your heart for others is gold -- allow it to flourish. Be humble and lead through transparency. Your vulnerability fosters honest communication and trust, strengthening the warriors under your leadership.

My dear brothers and sisters, take note of this: Everyone should be quick to listen, slow to speak and slow to become angry...
James 1:19, NIV

Listen Like a Warrior

God has the answers – are you listening? One of the most valuable lessons we can learn from the Word of God is to listen first.

God entrusted His most precious work to ordinary everyday people, obedient followers, and scribes for God's Kingdom.

Today, thousands of years later, the children of God are still being led by His Holy Word.

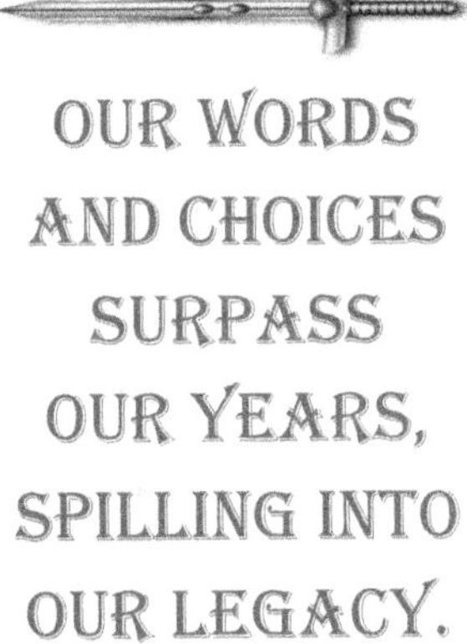

Our obedience to what God has for His children carries levels of blessings outlasting our existence. Our words and choices surpass our years, spilling into our legacy.

Warrior, you have the assignment to be still, not quick to speak, and let the wisdom of the Word seep in. When you have something to say, be the person who carries the weight of God's divine wisdom upon your lips.

If any of you lacks wisdom, you should ask God, who gives generously to all without finding fault, and it will be given to you.
James 1:5, NIV

Accomplish Like a Warrior

A warrior fights through difficult situations to finish her task. When the Pharaoh ordered all Hebrew boys to be murdered, the mother of Moses was determined that her son would live and not die. Jochebed dared to defy the command, but trusted God to accomplish His will for Moses' life (Exodus 2).

Having a spirit of excellence is what defines you and sets you apart from everyone else. It's time to rise up and become the winning warrior God created you to be. No longer allow fear and doubt to rule over trust and faith, consuming your thoughts. Speak to yourself and take the stance to no longer delay your dreams.

State this prayer over your life:

Heavenly Father, You are the way maker, and I put my trust in You. In Jesus Name, Amen.

Today, arm yourself, using the weapon of the Word to your advantage in battle.

This is what the Lord says to you: "do not be afraid or discouraged because of this vast army. For the Battle is not yours, but God."

2 Chronicles 20:15, NIV

Fight Like a Warrior

I thank You, Abba Father, for fighting my battles. Because of You, I am victorious. I will not give in. I declare today that I will not surrender to my fear, anxiety, or exhaustion. You prepared the Israelites to win their battles not by sharpening their swords or creating lavish tactics to overcome the enemy. They overcame by worshiping the one true God. For when they praised on the battlefield, their enemies were scattered (2 Chronicles 20:22).

God will fight for you because the battle is not yours but His. Praise Him when you are warring against the attacks and distractions of the enemy.

Your greatest weapons lie within your praise.

YOUR GREATEST WEAPONS AGAINST THE ENEMY LIE WITHIN YOUR PRAISE.

But now I urge you to keep up your courage, because not one of you will be lost; only the ship will be destroyed.
Acts 27:22, NIV

Courage Like a Warrior

Seasons come and go. We must garner the courage to sustain our faith in the Lord to trek each one. You are a treasure, strong and free! It takes grit to leave abuse and toxic characteristics to make life changes. I salute you today, brave Warrior. Storms may try to catapult fear into your heart, but you are not at the mercy of the torrential winds of chaos. Remind your soul to stay steady, for God is your shield and strength through uncertainties (Psalm 28:7).

Moments before becoming shipwrecked, the Apostle Paul encouraged his shipmates, "But now I urge you to keep up your courage, because not one of you will be lost; only the ship will be destroyed" (Acts 27:22, NIV). The angel of the Lord spoke the message to Paul, making him able to prophesy and inject faith-filled courage before the disaster threatened his people. Today, I prophesy a similar message to your heart – *Keep up your courage; you will not be lost, dear Warrior.*

*A gentle answer turns
away wrath,
but a harsh word stirs
up anger.*
Proverbs 15:1, NIV

Gentle Like a Warrior

How we speak to others is one of the most valuable tools, weapons, and influences we can carry. Our words can either kill or revitalize people's spirits, so we must not be careless with what we say (Proverbs 18:21).

The message we express and the tone we carry into someone's ears can be the tipping point between giving up or going on strong. Kindness is a Superfruit of the Spirit – a beautiful superpower (Galatians 5:22).

Choose your words wisely and convey your thoughts gently to others and yourself. Your own soul is listening to what you say.

So, today, speak life into circumstances; tell the story of faith and hope for tomorrow.

But you belong to God, my dear children. You have already won a victory over those people, because the Spirit who lives in you is greater than the Spirit who lives in the world.
1 John 4:4, NLT

Excel Like a Warrior

What is in you is greater than all that the world offers. Your Heavenly Father created you with purpose and for a purpose. You are not an accident; you are God's first choice to fulfill your assignment (Psalm 138:8).

If you knew that you were already going to win a race, would you go into the race feeling defeated?

Absolutely not! In like manner, this life may feel hard, but it has not beaten you. As you read this, I declare you are excelling more than you can imagine.

OWN YOUR IDENTITY IN CHRIST AS A CHILD OF GOD, FOR YOU ARE AMAZING, POWERFUL, AND PERFECTLY MADE.

Are you your worst critic? Don't be. You are chosen for victory through the Spirit of God living in you. Own your identity in Christ as a child of God, for you are amazing, powerful, and perfectly made.

"I am the Alpha and the Omega," says the Lord God, "who is, and who was, and who is to come, the Almighty."
Revelation 1:8, NIV

Worship Like a Warrior

I lift up my hands in a sign of surrender to You, oh Lord. Worthy, worthy are You, oh Lord. I celebrate Your goodness and raise a hallelujah of ultimate praise to Your name, Jehovah. Today I rejoice, giving You glory for the marriage of the Lion and the Lamb to Your Holy bride, the church. I will worship You at all times -- the days when I feel on top of the world and the dire days where my knees cannot hit the ground fast enough.

My life on this earth is Yours. Grateful, my heart calls out to You. I will declare Your faithfulness in the land of the living. I give You my hallelujah, the ultimate praise of Your glory.

Let me join the angels singing in constant awe of Your wonder – "Holy, Holy, Holy is the Lord God Almighty. The One who is, who was and is to come. Amen."

You, dear children, are from God and have overcome them, because the one who is in you is greater than the one who is in the world.
1 John 4:4, NIV

Activate Like a Warrior

Satan prowls like a thief in the night, trying to steal, kill and destroy (John 10:10). When the enemy is prowling around you, and you can feel the attacks of his darkness, there is only one thing to do -- activate the promises of God's Word over your life.

Your words carry power when you speak what God said. You have the power to set into action the promises of God. Through Christ, your Heavenly Father has already overcome the enemy, for He has overcome the world (John 16:33). His power is tremendous and resides within you. Because He is in you, you carry that same power.

Today, declare the Word of God over your life and activate the power of God to destroy the lies of the enemy.

Speak up for those who cannot speak for themselves, for the rights of all who are destitute. Speak up and judge fairly; defend the rights of the poor and needy.
Proverbs 31:8-9, NIV

Advocate Like a Warrior

Christ, the ultimate warrior, paid the price and sacrificed His own life so we can be free from shame, hurt, pain, and sin. When humanity was broken and unworthy, God the Father loved us. When we placed ourselves in bad situations, He sent His Son to be our Savior.

Hebrews 7:25 reminds us, "*He is able also to save forever those who draw near to God through Him, since He always lives to make intercession for them.*" Jesus Christ's resurrection solidified a position at the Father's right hand to intercede on our behalf, being our ultimate advocate.

Because Christ has shown us over and over again what true advocacy is, we too must garner the responsibility and pay it forward. Thankfully, we do not need to die on a cross for all humanity. Yet when we see injustices, we must advocate for others. Thank God, Jesus never stops interceding for us. He always takes a fighting stance for those who need mercy, justice, and healing.

"Yet in all these things we are more than conquerors through Him who loved us."
Romans 8:37, NKJV

Built Like a Warrior

Are you ready to overcome the challenges of the enemy? The Holy Spirit makes us aware of the enemy's works, and Paul speaks clearly about the challenges of the "last days" (2 Timothy 3).

In the recent pandemic, the world experienced hopelessness, confusion, and death. We need to remember that God is more powerful than any enemy or hardship, and He equips us to overcome.

You are built to be a warrior, not falling under the pressures of this world. You will not cave under the crisis of your circumstances. You are more than a conqueror. You were built to handle adversities and thrive through your trials.

The Holy Spirit is your comforter, helping you endure the challenges of these latter days, giving you power, love, and protection under His almighty wings (Hebrews 5:14).

For you created my
inmost being; you knit me
together in my mother's
womb. I praise you
because I am fearfully and
wonderfully made; your
works are wonderful,
I know that full well.
Psalm 139:13–14, NIV

Beautiful Like a Warrior

Our society has created a culture of stereotypes. Before posting on socials, we may filter and alter our photos because of some twisted idea of perfection with no comprehension of true beauty. I want to remind you that another's standard of attractiveness does *not* determine your beauty.

You are the idea of a Creator who makes no mistakes. He is flawless, which means your design is intentional and beautiful.

Today, boldly accept the inward and outward beauty bestowed on you by your Heavenly Father. Do not accept the insults and insecurities the enemy has tried to throw your way. Instead, remember how God took His time to knit you together from His heavenly throne room, most fearfully and wonderfully.

You are bold, courageous, and more beautiful than you think!

Two are better than one, because they have a good return for their labor: If either of them falls down, one can help the other up. But pity anyone who falls and has no one to help them up.
Ecclesiastes 4:9–10, NIV

Accountable Like a Warrior

Make this year more successful than the rest. How? In a nutshell, make yourself accountable. Ask God to connect you to the right person to support you in achieving your goals.

It's okay to say, *I've tried it on my own. It doesn't work. Now, I will finish the race with You, Lord, and another warrior by my side. I realize the joy I will have in celebrating the win in my life because I will not be on this journey alone.*

Whether you need to commit to losing weight, gaining faith, or something else, an accountability partner can strengthen you toward your goals. Ask the Lord to reveal a trustworthy person in your life who will be encouraging and hold you to your commitments.

"Teacher, which is the
great commandment in
the Law?" and he said
to him, "You shall love
the Lord your God with
all your heart and with
all your soul and with
all your mind." This
is the great and first
commandment. And a
second is like it: 'You
shall love your neighbor
as yourself.' On these two
commandments depend all
the Law and the Prophets."
Matthew 22:36-40, ESV

Love Like a Warrior

My God, how could You love me so unconditionally? You even gave Your life for me so that I can be free, be healed, and spend eternity in Your presence. Because You first loved me, I will always strive to love others. Help me never to walk past a person in need and do nothing. Make my Spirit aware of those who are hurting. I humbly ask that You use me as a vessel of Your love to those in need -- my family, my children, my coworkers, and those in my community. You embrace me with Your Heavenly love; now allow me to show others how powerful, graceful, and accepting You are, God. A warrior's love is strong enough to forgive, even in challenging situations. May I show Your love to all those around me for the rest of my days.

Today, abandon that evil grip and allow God's charge over your life, fearless Warrior.

Therefore encourage
(admonish, exhort)
one another and edify
(strengthen and build up)
one another, just as you
are doing.
1 Thessalonians 5:11, AMPC

Empower Like a Warrior

One of the greatest weapons the enemy employs against the children of God is hopelessness. When hope is gone, we don't even bother to try. God sent His only Son to the earth to bring us hope (Titus 2:13). Today, we have the privilege of going to our Heavenly Father, recognizing that our dark days are not eternal. God empowered His children with an unbeatable defense against darkness -- HOPE!

THE BEST WAY TO LEAD IS TO EMPOWER OTHERS TO SUCCEED, JUST AS JESUS CHRIST DID FOR US.

Today, you are not living your yesteryears of pain; you have the advantage of living with hope for brighter days. Greater days are yet to come. As children of God, continue paying it forward. The power of empowering and encouraging others around you will sow seeds of truth, confidence, and expectation for the future. Warrior, our battles are not simply our own; we also battle for the lives around us. The best way to lead is to empower others to succeed, just as Jesus Christ did for us.

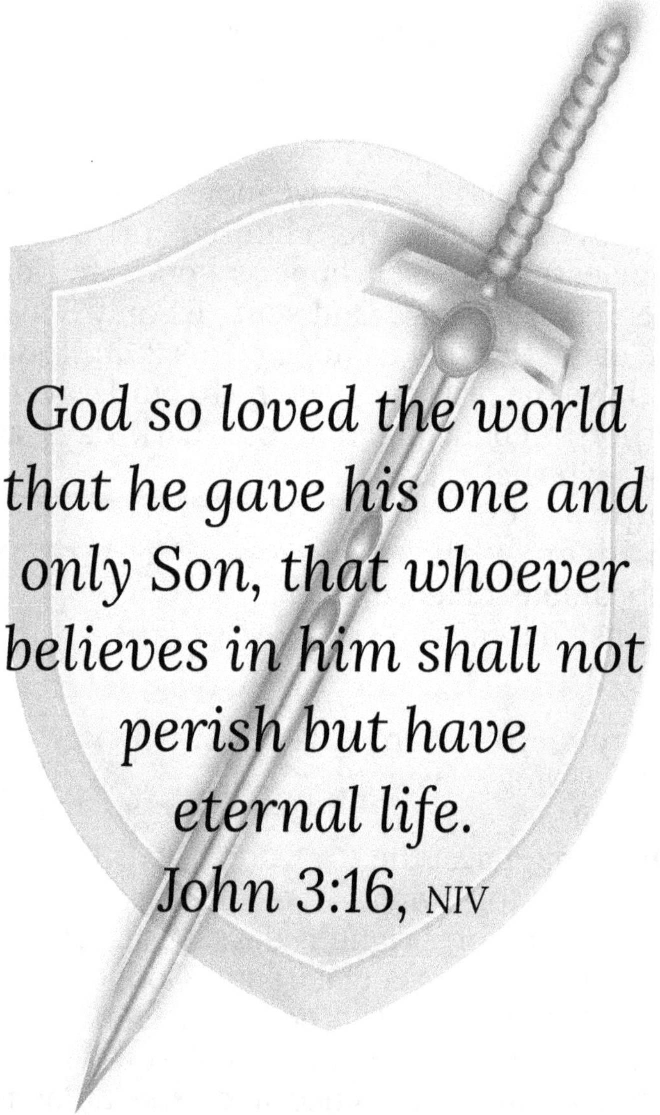

God so loved the world that he gave his one and only Son, that whoever believes in him shall not perish but have eternal life.
John 3:16, NIV

Decide Like a Warrior

Father, that dream You have given me, I will not put it down. I will not allow the cry of my current circumstances to drown out my dream. I believe You desire to fulfill every promise in Your Word. I will not give up. As a warrior, I will forge forward. God, I know that Your Word is a "lamp unto my feet and a light unto my path" (Psalm 119:105). I will not fear.

Doubt has no right in my life; Worry will turn her face from me. I will hold on and have faith in my God.

Father, as You did throughout the lives of every biblical hero, You will also make a way in my life. I trust You, God, and believe You for the breakthrough and the blessing in my life today. I have decided to follow You, Jesus, the Christ, and be led by my Heavenly Father.

*For we are God's handiwork, created in Christ Jesus
to do good works, which God prepared in advance for us to do.*
Ephesians 2:10, NIV

Inspire Like a Warrior

God created you by the inspired creative work of His thoughts. You bear His flawless image because a perfect idea formed a word on the Father's tongue – He spoke it and you came into existence. You are created in the image of a Creator, meaning inspiration is a natural characteristic of your being. C'mon dear one, you can inspire others.

In moments of hardship and seasons of ease, your life is a testament to God's sustaining power and goodness. Do not allow yourself to overlook the peaceful, beautiful moments. Look for opportunities to inspire others with what motivated you in the dark moments. *You can do this!*

Your story, your words are not weak. The simplest gesture of kindness, love, and positivity can wreak havoc on the hellish designs of the enemy, giving others the determination to break free. Be the hero in their story, or at least the apprentice of our heavenly hero.

...looking to Jesus, the founder and perfecter of our faith, who for the joy that was set before him endured the cross, despising the shame, and is seated at the right hand of the throne of God.

Hebrews 12:2, ESV

Achieve Like a Warrior

This is my year, Lord. This is my moment to reach new heights, experience opportunities I've never thought I could before.

Heavenly Father, with You on my side, I will not only dream about it, I will accomplish it. My mind is set upon You, Lord, "the author and finisher of my faith" (Hebrews 12:2).

Because I have surrendered my will, I am in position to learn more, earn more, and be more. Thank you for what Jesus Christ achieved on the cross, for He has and will forever be the most excellent example to me as a warrior for Your kingdom.

May all that I do be another level of giving glory, honor, and praise unto You, dear God.

But you are a chosen people, a royal priesthood, a holy nation, God's special possession, that you may declare the praises of him who called you out of darkness into his wonderful light.
1 Peter 2:9, NIV

Dress Like a Warrior

When Aaron was called into the office of the priesthood, God charged the Israelites with specific instructions, including what they must wear. His vestment reflected the consecrated office he carried. In like manner, when a princess is named Queen, her royal scepter and crown are unique and specific to her role in the monarchy.

Today, remember that God has called you and me into the royal priesthood of His kingdom. May we not allow a marred heart from past mistakes to mandate us unworthy of the Heavenly Father's love. I declare purification over your life and mind by the washing of Christ's blood over you.

People will know you are royalty by His love displayed through you (John 13:35). The Spirit of God dresses you and marks you as holy and chosen.

I can do all things through Christ who strengthens me. Philippians 4:13, NKJV

Do Like a Warrior

I can do all things through Christ who strengthens me. I can be a poised, strong, courageous, and anointed warrior for God's Kingdom because He is my strength. Culture, society, the norms I've known my entire life do not label me. God gave me an identity before the time of man. That is what defines me.

I am the mighty woman He created me to be. When I get up in the morning and when I lay my body to rest at night, the enemy will know that he cannot have his way with me. More incredible things are before me, and I am simply walking in the authority Christ gives me through His blood, shed on Calvary.

I AM A POISED, STRONG, COURAGEOUS, AND ANOINTED WARRIOR FOR GOD'S KINGDOM BECAUSE HE IS MY STRENGTH.

Today is a new day -- a day where I am making dreams happen because I am intentionally walking one more step towards them.

All the days of the afflicted are evil, but the cheerful of heart has a continual feast.

Proverbs 15:15, ESV

Celebrate Like a Warrior

When battles were won long ago, the victors rode horses into the city, waving their flags as onlookers threw flowers and cheered them.[3] When you have a victory in your life, you may not parade into town like a hero on horseback, but do not forget to acknowledge the achievement.

Donald Lawrence sings, "sometimes you have to encourage yourself." Learn to celebrate your wins and cherish the moments of accomplishments. Allow yourself to cheer your successes, small and epic. We serve a good Heavenly Father who wants the best for all of His children. Believe you are an exceptional child of God and are deserving of celebration. How are you speaking to yourself every day? Do not abuse yourself with toxic language. God has prepared a place for you because of how important you are to Him (John 14:3).

Today, begin a new day by speaking life into your being and applauding yourself. I say it's time to do a happy dance in honor of you!

Yet amid all these things we are more than conquerors through Him who has loved us. Romans 8:37, WNT

Conquer Like a Warrior

Sometimes we forget who we are because we lose focus of Who we belong to. Let me remind you, She-Warrior. God created you in His perfect image, making you more than a conqueror through His DNA. If you look down your family tree, you can see what similarities you have with your ancestors -- your nose, your body structure, your eyes and hair color, or some other trait. In like manner, you share the features of your Heavenly Father. He is the power and fortitude you need in life. Before your mother knew you in her womb, God already loved you. God's love conquered death for all humanity when He sent His only Son to save you and me (Romans 6:23). Imagine that! His love is so pure, bold, and mighty it creates a superpower for all those who need an injection of strength. Today, dear Warrior, remember *whose* you are and the spiritual genes you gained when you were born again. When you are in the middle of your battle, remember you are more than a conqueror. Stay Strong!

A man of many
companions may come
to ruin,
but there is a friend who
sticks closer
than a brother.
Proverbs 18:24, ESV

Friend Like a Warrior

Friends come, and friends go, but there is One who sticks closer to you than family. How beautiful to have a loving friend, a companion who will tell you the truth and have your back.

The gospel of John tells us Jesus was soon to become the martyr for all humanity; surely His disciples wondered how they would survive without their Master.

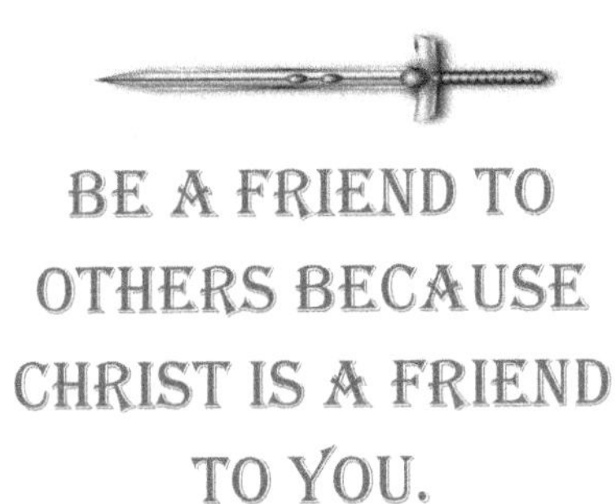

Jesus revealed that His Father would send the Comforter, His Spirit, to be with them when He departed this earth (John 14). The Holy Spirit does more than come alongside us – He dwells inside each of us. No matter what people enter or exit our circle, be a friend to them because Christ is a friend to you.

Give your burdens to the LORD, and he will take care of you. He will not permit the godly to slip and fall.
Psalm 55:22, NLT

Balance Like a Warrior

To be balanced is "to carry an even distribution of weight on all sides."[4] Imbalance can cause crashes, depression, frustrations, a slew of mental and physical illnesses. When our gratitude is out of proportion to our concerns, or we carry a load not meant for us to lift, we become uncertain and unstable.

To be warriors for God's Kingdom, we must allow God to shoulder our burdens. When we allow God to take on our troubles and stresses, we will fill our purpose, relationships, and health with calm and confidence.

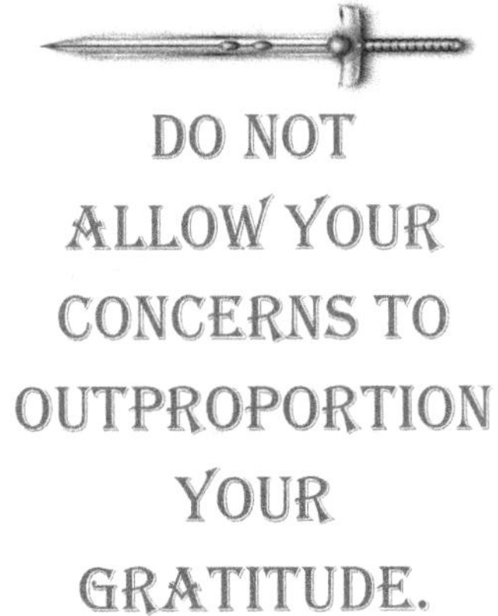

Today, I challenge you to cast your cares upon the Lord so that He can sustain your every move. Restore balance in your life and allow your Creator to do the heavy lifting for you.

But as it is written: "Eye has not seen, nor ear heard, Nor have entered into the heart of man The things which God has prepared for those who love Him."

1 Corinthians 2:9, NKJV

Delight Like a Warrior

The joy of the Lord is my strength. With confidence, I will believe every trial I am facing is temporary. I put my eyes upon the Lord, knowing He will give me the desires of my heart according to His will (Psalm 37:4). Today I am encouraged and strengthened. It is easy to trust in You, God, because Your Word says, "no eye has seen, no ear has heard, and no mind has imagined what you have prepared" for those that love You. And I love You with all my heart. You make me strong. Because of You, I will delight in this day as I praise You, Lord.

"for this day is holy to our Lord. Do not sorrow, for the joy of the LORD is your strength." (Nehemiah 8:10b, NKJV)

He drew me up from the pit of destruction, out of the miry bog, and set my feet upon a rock, making my steps secure.
Psalms 40:2, ESV

Adapt Like a Warrior

When unexpected circumstances arise, be flexible. Adjust to situations out of your control and refuse to be thrown off mission. Speak into your life, "*I will not lose my ability to think through this situation because my mind is set upon the Lord.*" When God bends you, He'll not break you. You are a Warrior!

Moses received clear instructions directly from God, yet he stubbornly refused to obey like many of us. Still, God ordered his steps, making him stronger through every pivot, completing his assignment from God (Exodus 14). Now *you* decide – will you be blindsided and thrown off balance, or will you adapt and *grow* with the flow?

Commit now to never settle for comfortable remedies that delay your advancement; instead, embrace the challenges which are crucial to your relentless forward movement. Keep adapting and pivoting when God needs you to. It will pay off in the end.

So if the Son sets you free,
you will be free indeed.
John 8:36, NIV

Challenge Like a Warrior

Jesus drew a line in the sand before the accusers of a woman who committed a sinful act and was about to get stoned (Matthew 7). His love, grace, and compassion for her called to her heart. At that moment, the woman received an advocate.

Jesus will always be our advocate, meeting the attacks of the accuser. His love protects and challenges us to live a sinless and holy life.

JESUS HAS DRAWN A LINE IN THE SAND FOR YOU AND SET YOU FREE FROM YOUR PAST.

Our Savior wants more for us than a pit of oppression, fear, and hopelessness. A warrior meets the challenges of the Christian life with joyful obedience, knowing each choice brings growth and encouragement to others.

You are a testament to the strength found in Jesus; a saint in the eyes of God, and child of the King. Jesus has drawn a line in the sand for you and set you free from your past. *Where are your accusers?* Go and live the freedom you are given, for he who the Son sets free is truly free!

But as for you, be strong and do not give up, for your work will be rewarded.
Chronicles 15:7, NIV

Grit Like a Warrior

Because our Almighty Creator has formed you, you already have all the tools necessary within you to conquer all that lies ahead.

Today, I challenge you to build that tough-girl attitude; believe you *can* "do all things through Christ who strengthens" you (Philippians 4:13). Who told you what you hope for is impossible? After all, you serve a God who turns unachievable dreams into undeniable proof.

Look at the word *impossible* this way -- IM - POSSIBLE! God is the Great I Am; all you need to push forward with grit and resolve. Tell Satan, Not *today* & *not ever!*

YOU SERVE A GOD WHO TURNS UNACHIEVABLE DREAMS INTO UNDENIABLE PROOF.

Unflinching Warrior, you can do it. Believing for a miracle? Don't quit. Believing for a breakthrough? Don't quit. Believing for a job? Do not quit.

May the words of my mouth and the meditation of my heart be pleasing to you, O Lord, my rock and my redeemer.
Psalm 19:14, NLT

Communicate Like a Warrior

To the many warriors who may feel unheard, today is for you. No one understands you better than your Heavenly Father. He desires your interaction with Him from deep sorrow to sunshine-filled joy. You can run to Him any time, and He will fill you.

Warriors on the battlefield hone their talents and understand their weapons. Even the most skilled soldier would be quickly defeated without knowing the language of their commander.

When you are in the trenches, you must recognize the command either to advance and fight or hold steady and rest. When you interconnect with God, the more intimate you become, the greater your understanding will be of His nature and ways.

For where two or three are gathered together in my name, there am I in the midst of them.
Matthew 18:20, NKJV

Collaborate Like a Warrior

You are not created to fight alone. Before Jesus died on the cross, He told His disciples they would not be alone; God was sending the Comforter, the precious Holy Spirit, to guide them (John 15:26).

God does not expect us to live on our own strength. Like the disciples, we are collaborators with God's Spirit to do the work of God's Kingdom here on earth. When we join others in this Kingdom of God assignment, the Holy Spirit uses our unique skillsets for a united purpose.

If doing things alone is more comfortable to you because you are afraid of getting hurt, be encouraged today -- relationship is God's design. Remember, Jesus had His twelve, plus the Holy Spirit. Whatever you face in this season, do not take it on alone. It is time to collaborate and conquer.

Love is patient, love is kind. It does not envy, it does not boast, it is not proud. It does not dishonor others, it is not self-seeking, it is not easily angered, it keeps no record of wrongs. Love does not delight in evil but rejoices with the truth. It always protects, always trusts, always hopes, always perseveres.

1 Corinthians 13:4-7, NIV

Forgive Like a Warrior

One of the most profoundly beneficial moves we can make for our spiritual health is the decision to forgive. Today, gracious Warrior, choose not to allow anything to hold back your mental, spiritual and physical health.

Forgiveness starts within and is not dependent on the offender's apology or awareness. When we determine to forgive others and ourselves in our hearts, we narrow the chasm of bitterness the enemy uses to separate us from God's blessings (Ecclesiastes 7:9). He will keep you in darkness, ruminating on the hurt, closed off by bitter thoughts and pain. The depths of despair are real, but so is our Heavenly Father's profound love.

Never forget that God's love is patient. Release your dark, empty, intimate places to the Father, for He is waiting to continue making you whole.

But my life is worth nothing to me unless I use it for finishing the work assigned me by the Lord Jesus – the work of telling others the Good News about the wonderful grace of God.
Acts 20:24, NLT

Dream Like a Warrior

There is no dream too big or talent too small for God. If you believe the things you are good at are not significant, remember that He designed you to accomplish your dreams. The dream you carry in the depth of your heart is associated with the characteristics of what you are naturally good at.

Are you an entrepreneur in business? Creative or organized? Do you make others smile? Do spontaneity and adventure energize you, or do you enjoy a quiet conversation?

THERE IS NO DREAM TOO BIG OR TALENT TOO SMALL FOR GOD.

Whatever your unique qualities or preferences, you can be sure they are essential to carrying out God's assignment. My warrior, continue to dream and tie your instinctive talents to your beautiful vision. Please don't give up on it. As Paul stated in the book of Acts, every part is useful in finishing the work appointed to you by our Lord Jesus. Hope and dream and finish your work in God's great Kingdom plan.

*I instruct you in the way
of wisdom and lead you
along straight paths.*
Proverbs 4:11, NIV

Lead Like a Warrior

I will not fear the loneliness on the battlefield. I know I must go ahead to pave a path and set up camp. Even when no one is aware, I will keep the fire burning because I sense the responsibility of the task.

My passion pushes me toward the prize. I am not alone; God is with me, He is for me, and He loves me. I am a leader of righteousness, not a follower of envy, jealousy, or bewitching talk.

You, my Heavenly Father, instruct me, and I will not allow Your teaching to fall on deaf ears. I am created for Your Kingdom's sake, leading with humility, wisdom, and grace.

Give, and it will be given to you. A good measure, pressed down, shaken together and running over, will be poured into your lap. For with the measure you use, it will be measured to you.
Luke 6:38, NIV

Give Like a Warrior

Burnout is a hot topic of conversations in ministry and work environments, even when working with family. Burnout happens when we give beyond what we have in our reserves, causing us to become unable to sustain ourselves physically and emotionally.

God has given you all you need for today and more; He desires your overflow to stream to others. What is overflow? When we receive constant nourishment from God, we take in more than what we need for ourselves alone. The overflow is what remains to pour out on the daily to family, children, work, ministry, and other areas.

We can give freely without the spiritual deprivation that leads to burnout. Serving will not lead to collapsing if you take time to feed on, fill up, and run over from God's goodness.

This is what the LORD says: Do what is just and right. Rescue from the hand of the oppressor the one who has been robbed. Do no wrong or violence to the foreigner, the fatherless or the widow, and do not shed innocent blood in this place.
Jeremiah 22:3, NIV

Defend Like a Warrior

To boldly seek God's face is to boldly protect the innocence of His children. *Being* His children, we are to guard and defend our virtue and the purity of others.

Satan has perverted cultures, marring every passing generation with darkness and oppression. As warriors, we stand up against such things and become intercessors for victims of such cruelty (Proverbs 29:7). Some organizations and charities try to meet the needs of the abused and misused, but programs are not enough.

You are appointed to protect innocence by speaking up, stepping in, and creating healthy, safe environments for yourself and those around you. Are you a safe haven for others?

Today, do a self-check to become a secure, peaceful, God-filled atmosphere for others to grow and heal. A warrior guards her innocence and stands in the gap for others.

Endnotes
1   "Boss Definition & Meaning." Merriam-Webster, Merriam-Webster, https://www.merriam-webster.com/dictionary/boss.
2   "How to Stop Negative Self-Talk." Mayo Clinic, Mayo Foundation for Medical Education and Research, 21 Jan. 2020, https://www.mayoclinic.org/healthy-lifestyle/stress-management/in-depth/positive-thinking/art-20043950.
3   Oord, Christian. "The Maid of Orléans : How Joan of Arc Defeated the English." WAR HISTORY ONLINE, 27 Sept. 2019, https://www.warhistoryonline.com/instant-articles/maid-of-orleans-joan-of-arc.html.
4   "Balance Definition & Meaning." Merriam-Webster, Merriam-Webster, https://www.merriam-webster.com/dictionary/balance.

ALSO BY
ROSALINDA RIVERA

Dare to Begin Again Journal

Seductive Slayers of Success
(Whitaker House)

<u>The Wonder Series</u>
Wonder Women
Wonder Mom

Atrévete a Comenzar de Nuevo

Dare to Begin Again
(Whitaker House)

Coming Soon to the DARE family --
Dare to Begin Again Study Guide
for Groups and Individuals

Still to come in The Wonder Series
Wonder Wife
Wonder Kid

ABOUT THE AUTHOR

Rosalinda Rivera is outspoken and passionate about helping others change their lives and accomplish their dreams. She is a sought-after speaker by major companies, non-profits, and ministries around the world for her high energy, humorous, and down-to-earth, motivational style.

Host of the *Faith Fuel* podcast, Rosalinda is an internationally known speaker and author. Rosalinda served as Associate Producer on *Victor*, a movie about her father's journey from drugs and gangs to Jesus and redemption. Along with her husband, Carlos, Rosalinda is Executive Director of *New Life for Adults and Youth* headquartered in Virginia. For more than twenty-five years, Rosalinda has been reaching out to families in crisis, poverty, and hopelessness to bring them hope and a positive future.

Known as a "Change Strategist," Rosalinda has been a featured presenter and ministered across the U.S. and throughout the world. From the White House to the local community, she is nationally recognized for her impact in bringing hope to the hopeless. Rosalinda was appointed to the Board of Governors of the National Association of Nonprofit Organizations and Executives, headquartered in Washington, DC.

Rosalinda and her husband, Carlos, are Pastors at *New Life Outreach* in Richmond, Virginia. They have three children: Alana, Gabriel, and Victor.